It's a Wrap!

*How to Draw Fabric Folds
for Realistic Clothing and Drapery*

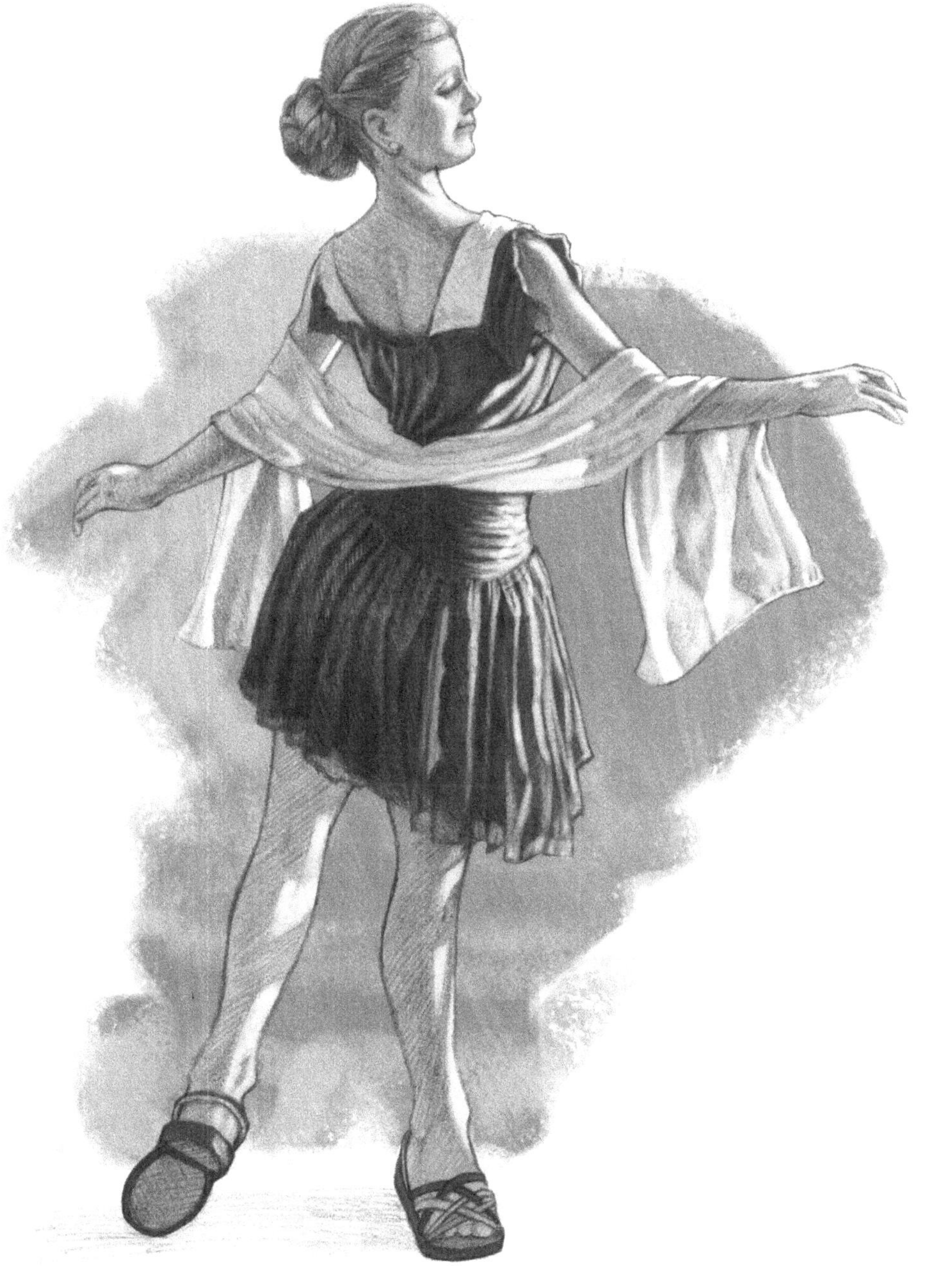

Written and Illustrated by Benjamin Hummel

CHERISHED SOLUTIONS, LLC / GOLDEN, COLORADO

DEDICATION

To all the artists — may you fully embrace your creative journey.

Join the movement at **ArtStudioNation.com**

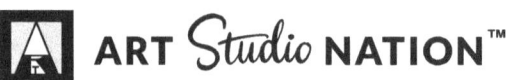

ART *Studio* NATION™

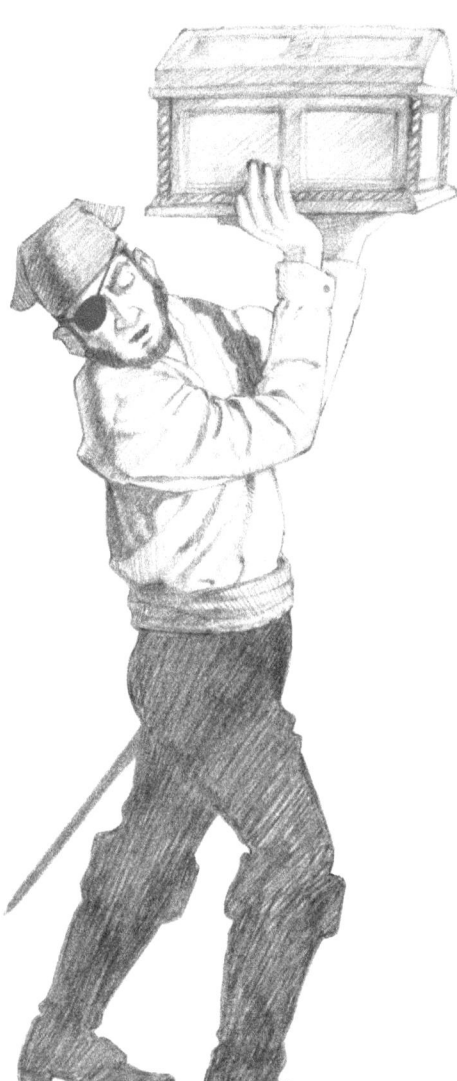

Cherished **Solutions**™

TABLE OF CONTENTS

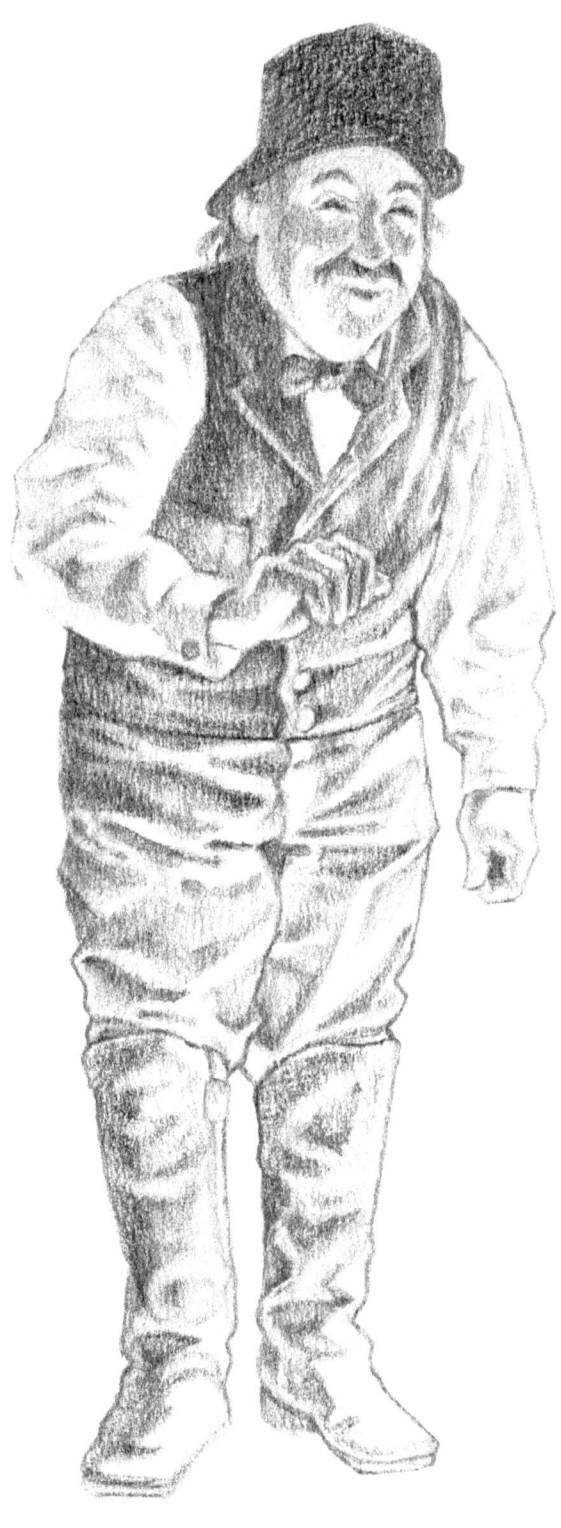

INTRODUCTION

Folds on fabric and clothing can sometimes be the most neglected part of working on a piece of art. Oftentimes as artists, we approach what the fabric is doing as an afterthought. Or we believe there is so much complexity in the piece that we become intimidated. At this point, we either give up or we hurry and sketch in some random lines hoping that will somehow do the trick.

But here's the problem. When folds are rendered incorrectly, it can ruin an otherwise perfect piece of art. Like everything else, folds have a very specific anatomy, and putting lines in the wrong places will make the piece look lumpy or lack form.

The good news is, once you understand why drapery acts the way that it does, you'll be better equipped to anticipate it and observe it correctly. Knowing what you are observing will allow you to correctly translate that into your drawings. This makes drawing easier, freeing you up to be more expressive and creative in your work.

The instructions in this book are a detailed breakdown of the structure of folds. These notes are based on my understanding, observations, and teachings through the years, finally collected in single place.

Folds do not have to be intimidating. With a little knowledge backed by attention to detail, you too can achieve masterful flowing drapery in your artwork.

THREE KEY POINTS ABOUT FOLDS

1. Folds are three-dimensional

First and foremost, folds are three-dimensional. Remember this! This concept is vital in understanding how to realistically see and draw folds. I cannot stress this fact enough. When you are looking at folds in fabric, you are actually looking at three-dimensional form. Folds are arranged in a conglomeration of a variety of shapes, all connected together as fabric bunches up and moves around. These shapes are the basic shapes we have come to be familiar with from our earliest drawing classes— cylinders, cones, and triangles. Frequently, we'll see a lot of artists represent folds in fabric simply as lines. That's okay, as long as those lines are the correct lines, and as long as they are actually representing the outer edges of formed shapes.

We artists often find folds difficult to draw since there appears to be a dizzying amount of lines moving all over the place. But, when you start to see these lines as the contours of larger blocks of shapes, the drapery suddenly becomes more simplified. For example, three lines by themselves are three different contours an artist has to think about and observe. However, three lines that are the edges of a triangular area can be seen as a single shape, simplifying what the artist's mind has to process.

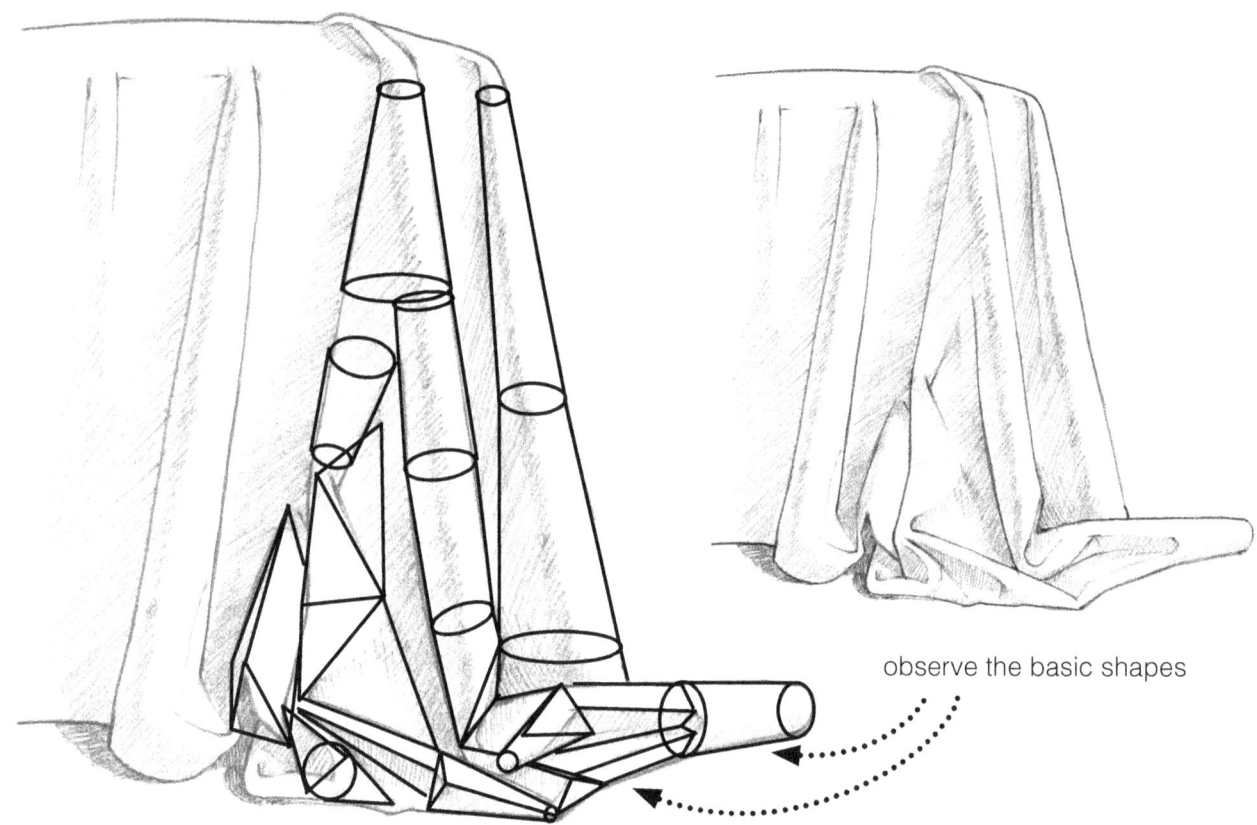

observe the basic shapes

Once you start to grasp that the folds you are looking at are constructed from a series of multiple three-dimensional shapes, the second most important element to understand is that these shapes are actually connected to one another. It is the interconnectivity of the different fold shapes that makes the clothing or drapery appear realistic. If you lose this in your drawing, you'll end up with a bunch of lines that don't make a whole lot of sense.

Start by trying to see within the folds some of the basic shapes you learned about in perhaps some of your beginning drawing classes. Specifically, the three most common basic forms you'll see in drapery are the cylinder, the cone, and the tent or pyramid. All of the rules about lighting on the cylinder, cone and triangular form remain true,

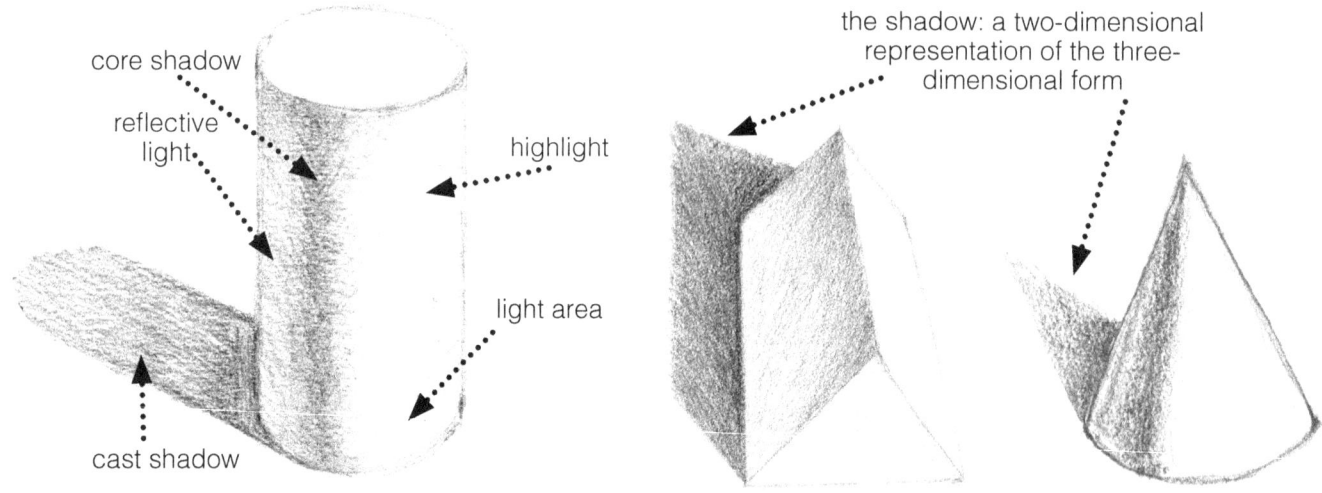

core shadow

reflective light

highlight

light area

cast shadow

the shadow: a two-dimensional representation of the three-dimensional form

even in your drapery. If you can remember how to do shading on a basic cylinder, half your work is done.

Remember the different parts of shading: light area, shadow area, core shadow, cast shadow, reflective light, highlights, and basic planes and their shadows. The rules of shading remain true whether you are observing and drawing from a wooden block, or recognizing it in your drapery.

As you sit down to draw drapery, look for these shapes. Watch the shapes as they shift and move and change. Observe where they connect and how they move to the next shape. All of those shapes will have areas of light and areas of shadow based on the basic form of the shape. Those shapes will cast shadows onto other basic forms. Remember the rules about cast shadows: ***a cast shadow replicates the shape that casts it as well as the surface onto which it is cast.***

In the case of drapery, this can get tricky, as the large combination of shapes can really affect how those cast shadows appear and you can get some very interesting shadow shapes as a result. However, always keep in the back of your mind exactly how those shadows are created and look for those shapes as you go about rendering them.

As I discuss in other drawing books, I often find it helpful to draw a line to indicate the edge of the shadow area. It helps me look more specifically for the varying shapes the shadows create and I can then quickly add tone into my shadow area, keeping it distinct from the light. When this has been completed, I can go back with more detail, as needed.

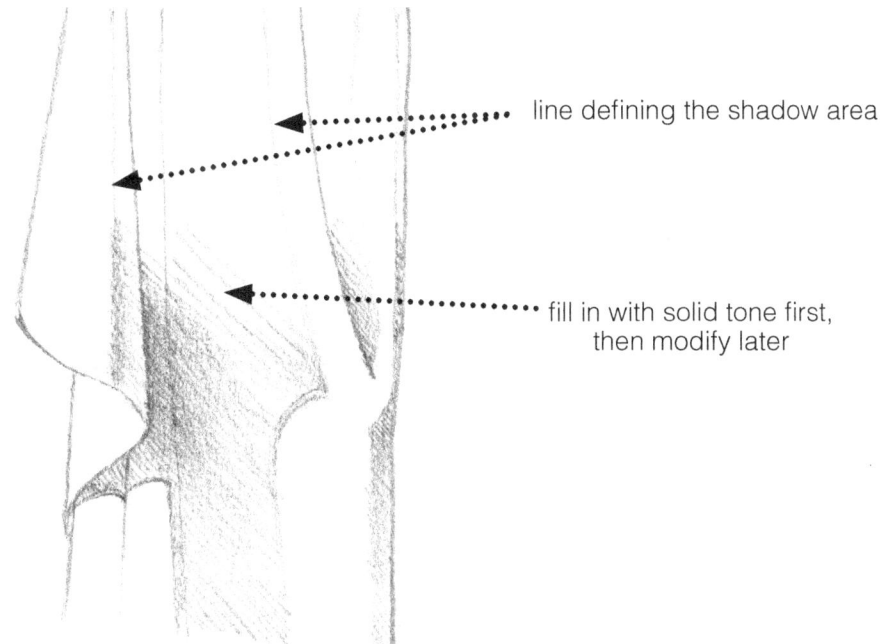

line defining the shadow area

fill in with solid tone first,
then modify later

As you begin to approach the folds in drapery as three-dimensional forms, you'll see measurable improvements in the realism of your art.

2. Folds follow the form of the object that the fabric is covering.

This sounds pretty self-explanatory, but it's amazing how many miss this when they get to their drawing. Drapery and folds help reveal the shape underneath. The drapery cannot cut into the rounded form underneath... and the folds cannot either. If the object is rounded, the folds of the drapery will wrap around the object in a rounded fashion. If the object is more complex, like the wet drapery sculptures of Hellenistic Greece, again, the linear quality of the folds will move in the direction of the more complex object. And if you were to throw a large cloth over a ceramic goose (see below), well, the result is that the drapery will be influenced by the form of the ceramic goose.

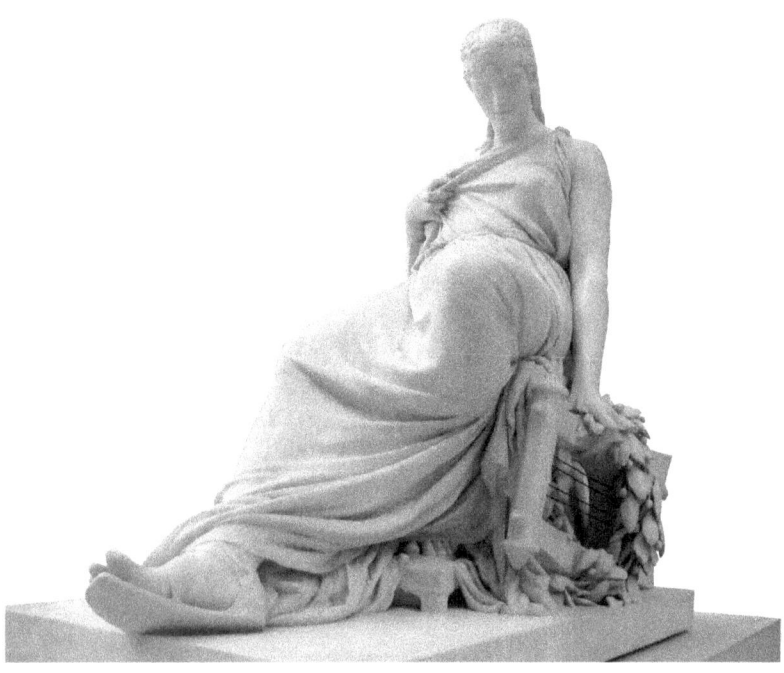

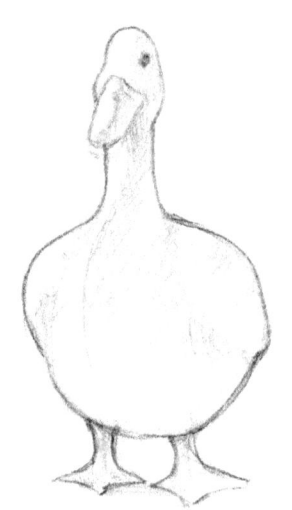

This is a ceramic goose drawn first without drapery, and then covered with drapery. Notice how the folds move AROUND the shape of the goose, and don't cut into it.

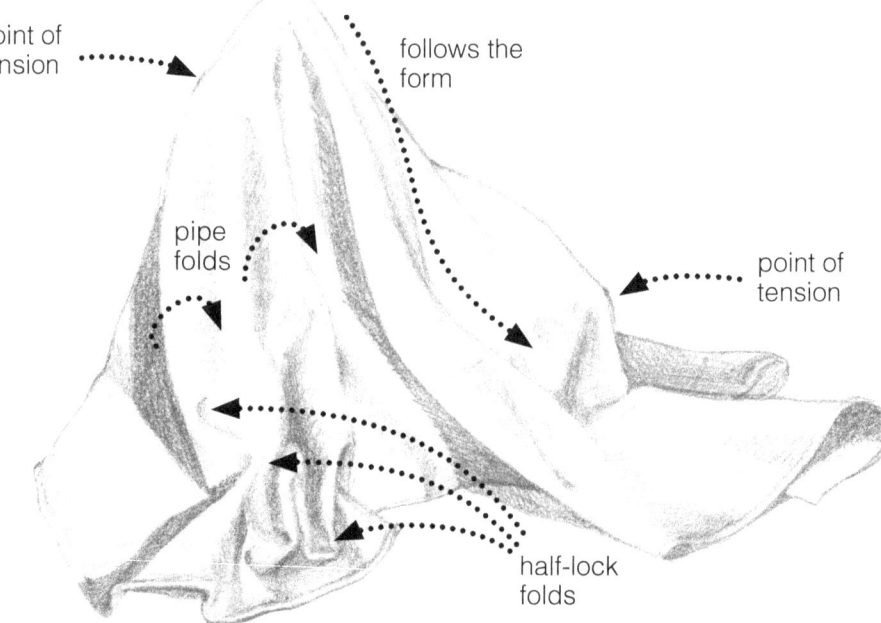

point of tension

follows the form

pipe folds

point of tension

half-lock folds

3. Folds move away from the direction of tension points.

Everything about a fold including its shape and the direction it moves, is the result of tension points. If you are really trying to understand what's going on with a particular piece of drapery or fabric, first try and figure out what's going on with the tension points. In order to help simplify this idea, I've broken it down into four different types of tension points. All folds will be influenced by one or more of these four different types of tension points.

ONE: Gravity Tension

Folds are subject to gravity, just like everything else. Flopped loosely over an object, the drapery will fall away from that object at the different points of tension. These are the points that are the most prominent, or outward points of that object. From there, gravity will pull the fabric down until it either hangs in space, or hits another surface, which then will change the tension.

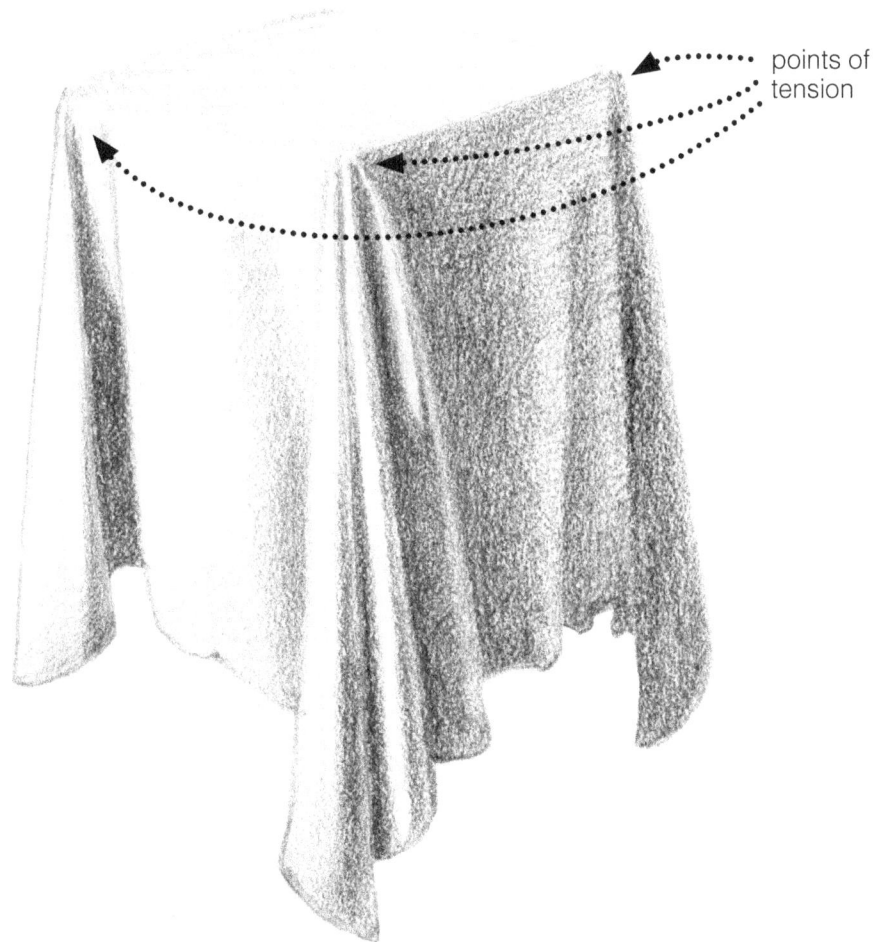

points of
tension

TWO: Bunch Tension

This is where the fabric falls upon itself and the folds start to bunch up on top of each other. The tension in this case is the fabric itself, as it zigzags back and forth trying to find room in a crowded area. Oftentimes this bunching can be caused by gravity, but sometimes fabric in a pulled-up sleeve will do the same thing. Anytime fabric has been gathered together, sewn together or compressed, or falls on top of itself, bunching will occur. The shapes of the resulting folds made by bunch tension are unique and will be discussed in the *Types of Folds* section.

THREE: Stress Tension

This is usually observed in clothing, and is the result of the figure or the form pulling the fabric in a certain direction. When this happens, it creates a stress tension point. Whether it's the elbow in a sleeve, or a bent knee, the one observable factor to folds made by stress tension is that they will all radiate out from that point of tension. Often there will be primary points of tension and then secondary points of tension.

Look for those points of tension in your drawing. Then move your lines from that point. Make sure it's clear that your folds are emerging from that point of tension. Make sure that it is very clear that your folds are coming from that point of tension. Sometimes it is helpful to simply find the points of stress tension and to draw radiating lines first. Later, you can try and see how the folds fit along those lines. This is how you can keep your folds aligned properly with your points of stress tension.

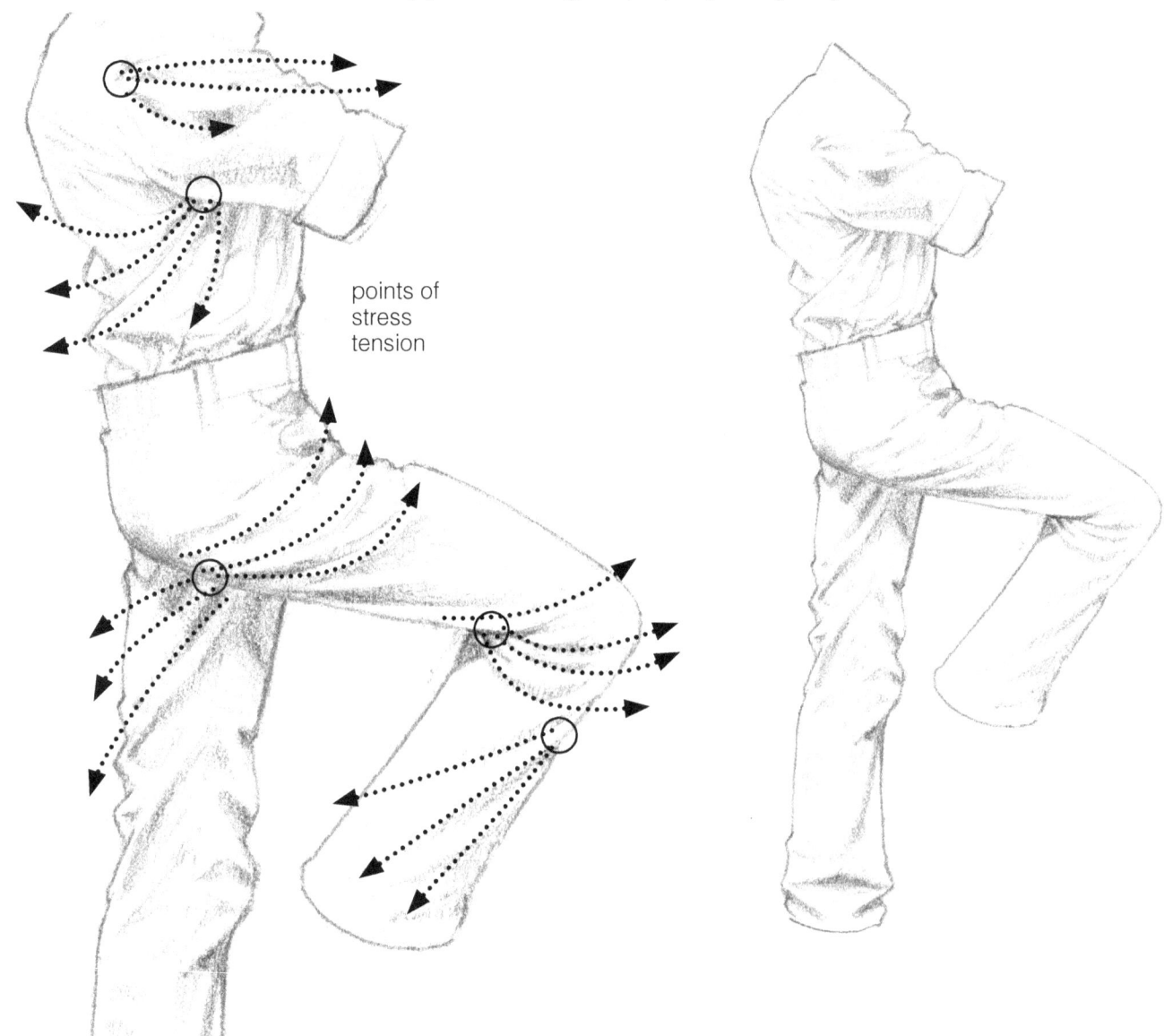

points of
stress
tension

FOUR: Movement Tension

Finally, we must address what happens when there is movement of the form underneath the drapery. The most observable example of this is during the twirl. The twirl responds to the movement of the body, but in a delayed manner, both when the form starts its movement, and when it finishes. The further away from the body the fabric is, the more exaggerated the delay. This can be tracked almost parabollically as a line starting from the form and then flowing away from the movement of the form toward the original starting position of the figure.

That may sound all mathematical and jargoned, but what does it mean practically? It means you can track the motion of the body through lines in the fabric that twist in the same radial direction of the form. These lines start where the fabric is closest to the body, and curve in the opposite direction of the twirl or movement of the body.

It also means that once the person has abruptly stopped his or her motion, the fabric will continue to move in that direction until it wraps around the body and eventually falls back down flat, obeying the demands of gravity. This back and forth can create all sorts of interesting criss-crossing of lines, and can be fun to observe and try to get down on paper. Just remember, however, that even in motion, all of the rules of folds discussed earlier still apply, such as the three-dimensionality of folds, tension point rules, and the wrapping of the form.

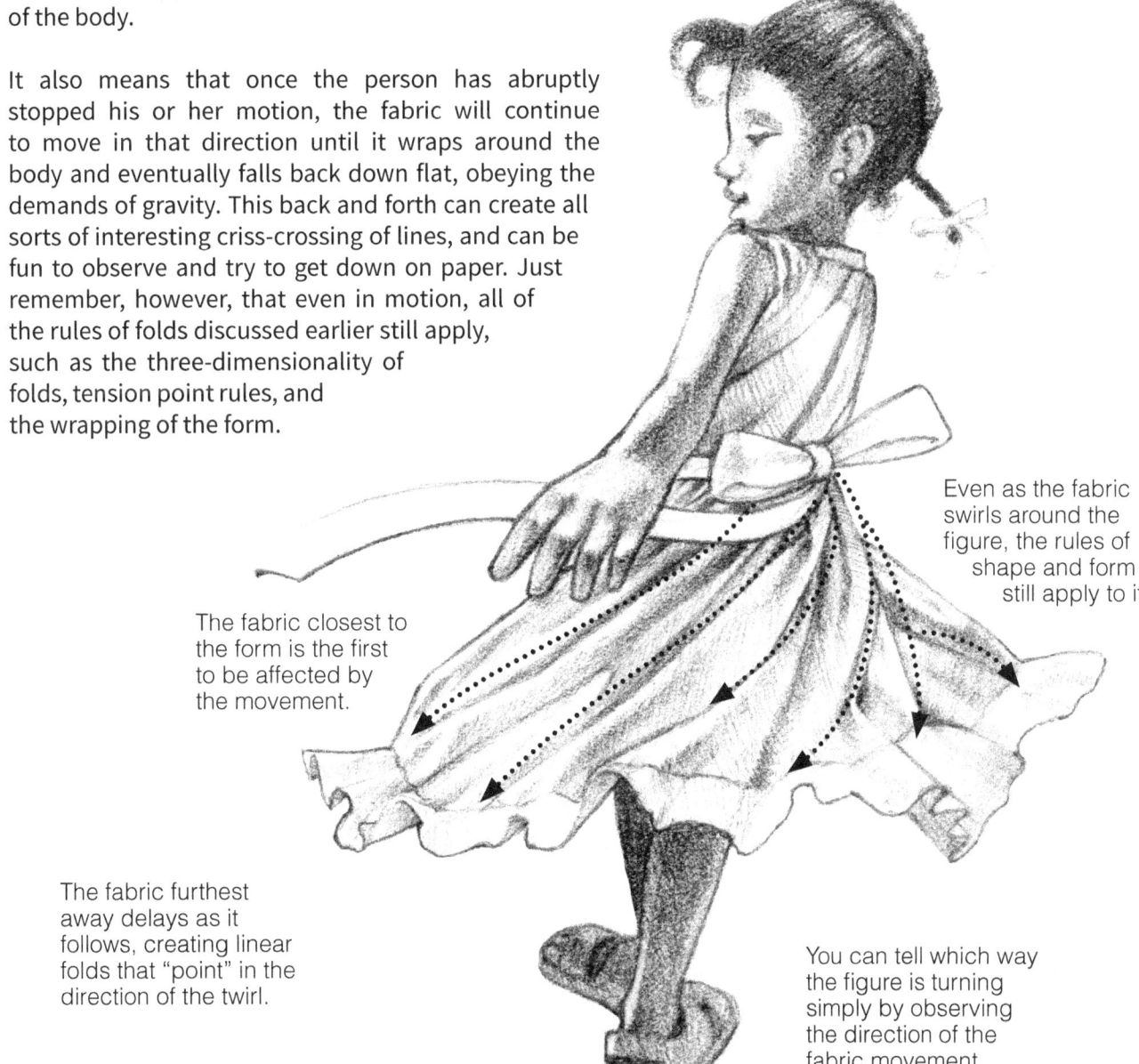

The fabric closest to the form is the first to be affected by the movement.

The fabric furthest away delays as it follows, creating linear folds that "point" in the direction of the twirl.

Even as the fabric swirls around the figure, the rules of shape and form still apply to it.

You can tell which way the figure is turning simply by observing the direction of the fabric movement.

It's a Wrap! How to Draw Folds for Realistic Clothing and Drapery

12

FIVE: Invisible Tensions

Flags are unique in the fact that they are slightly different than fabric draped over an object or wrapped around a form. However, the rules that we've just learned still do apply. The only real difference is that instead of the fabric being affect by something seen, such as a human being or a ceramic goose, it's being affected by the unseen, namely, the wind.

The first key to remember when drawing flags is to make sure the lines connect. As the fabric flaps over upon itself, you can actually trace from where the fabric begins to turn to the end of the fold at the other side of the flag, or until the fold flattens back up into open fabric. Sometimes it is helpful to draw through the fabric to make sure connections are correct, which will give your flag more realism.

The second key to drawing flags is that they incorporate all the different types of tension we have been talking about. There is stress tension at the point where the flag pulls away from the pole. There is gravity tension as the flag falls from the pole. And there is movement tension as it flaps in the wind. It is the ultimate challenge to try to visually see and incorporate these different points of tension into a cohesive piece of fabric. Fortunately, as it is a square piece of fabric, that makes things easier … until, of course, you start putting designs on the fabric.

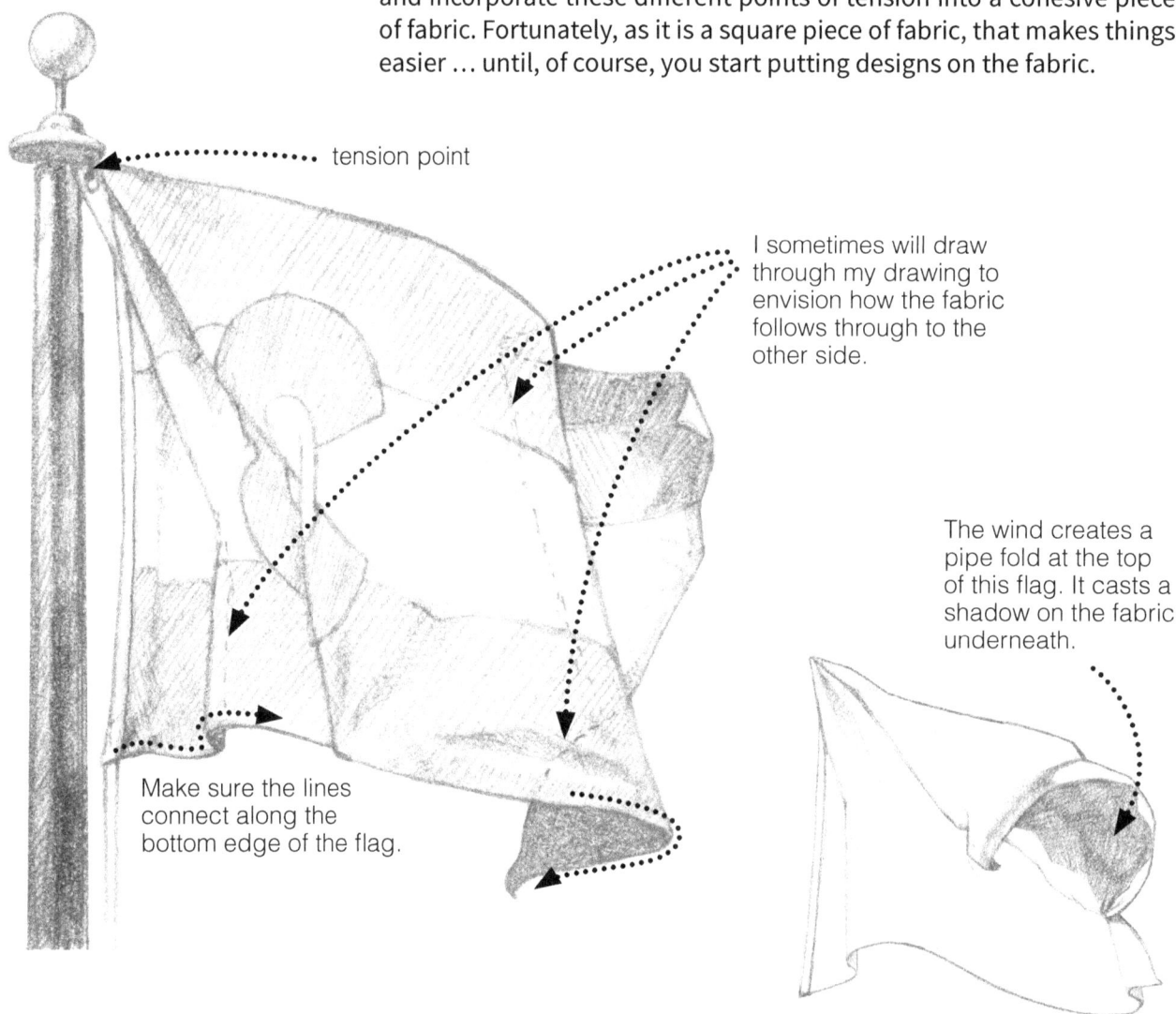

tension point

I sometimes will draw through my drawing to envision how the fabric follows through to the other side.

The wind creates a pipe fold at the top of this flag. It casts a shadow on the fabric underneath.

Make sure the lines connect along the bottom edge of the flag.

Drawing the designs of the flag doesn't have to be complicated. You just have to remember to have those designs follow the movement and the form of the flag and its folds. Sometimes a flag with a strong linear design can prove helpful, as the design helps us better "see" the movement of the flag, with our eyes following those lines from one end of the flag to the other.

Follow the lines of your design, even as they disappear behind the folds and flaps of the flag. Again, draw through the flag if you need to. And with all of this, I cannot emphasize enough the importance of pure observation. When you begin to truly see what is occurring, it will become easier to translate that into your drawing.

At times, you may find yourself in a situation where the light actually is shining from behind the flag, giving it an illuminated quality. Keep in mind that the more the fabric bunches up, the less light comes through, and the darker in value that area becomes. Also remember that around the edges and where the fabric hems will also go darker. Once you understand this, illuminating that flag can be quite a dramatic effect.

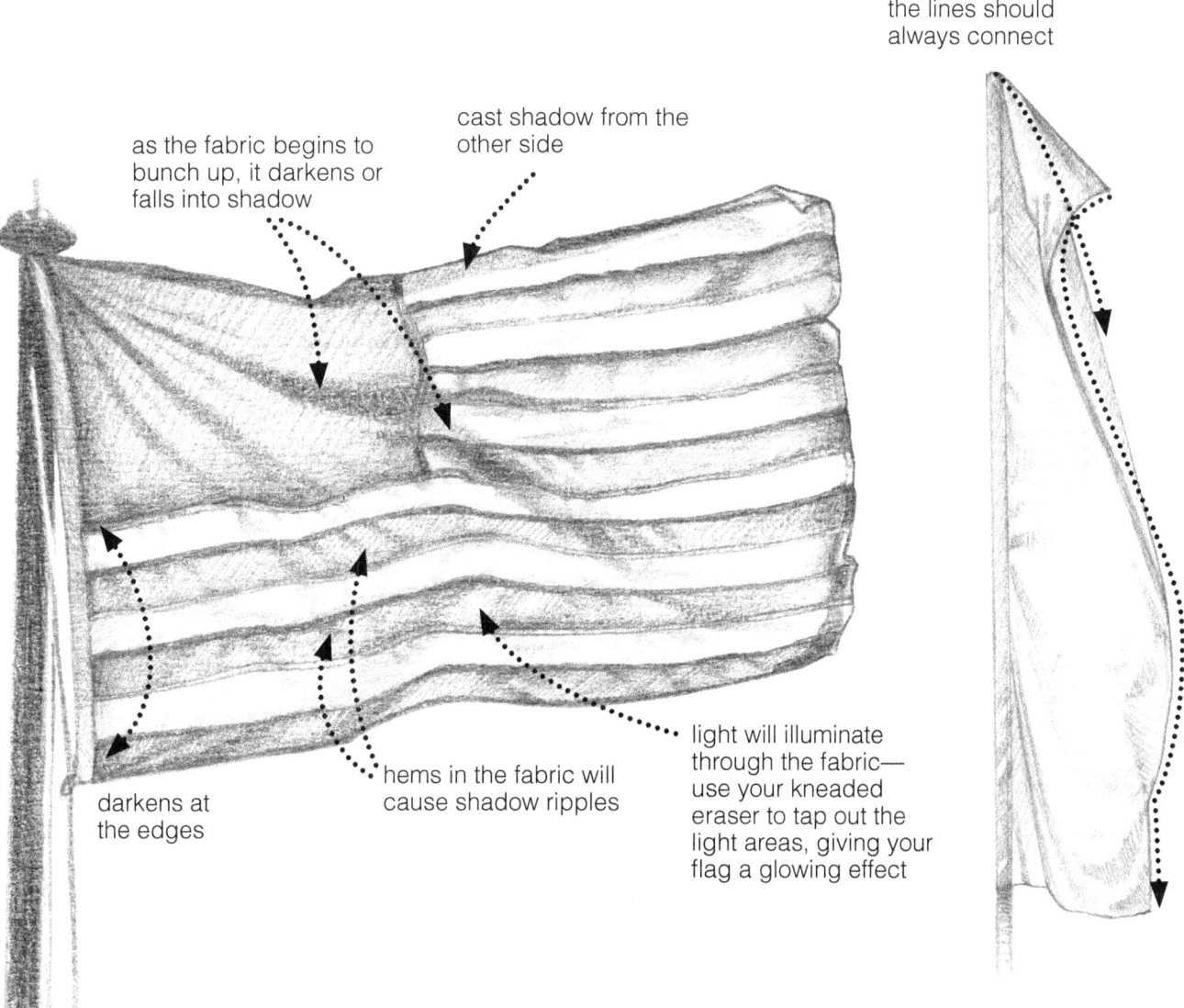

the lines should always connect

as the fabric begins to bunch up, it darkens or falls into shadow

cast shadow from the other side

darkens at the edges

hems in the fabric will cause shadow ripples

light will illuminate through the fabric— use your kneaded eraser to tap out the light areas, giving your flag a glowing effect

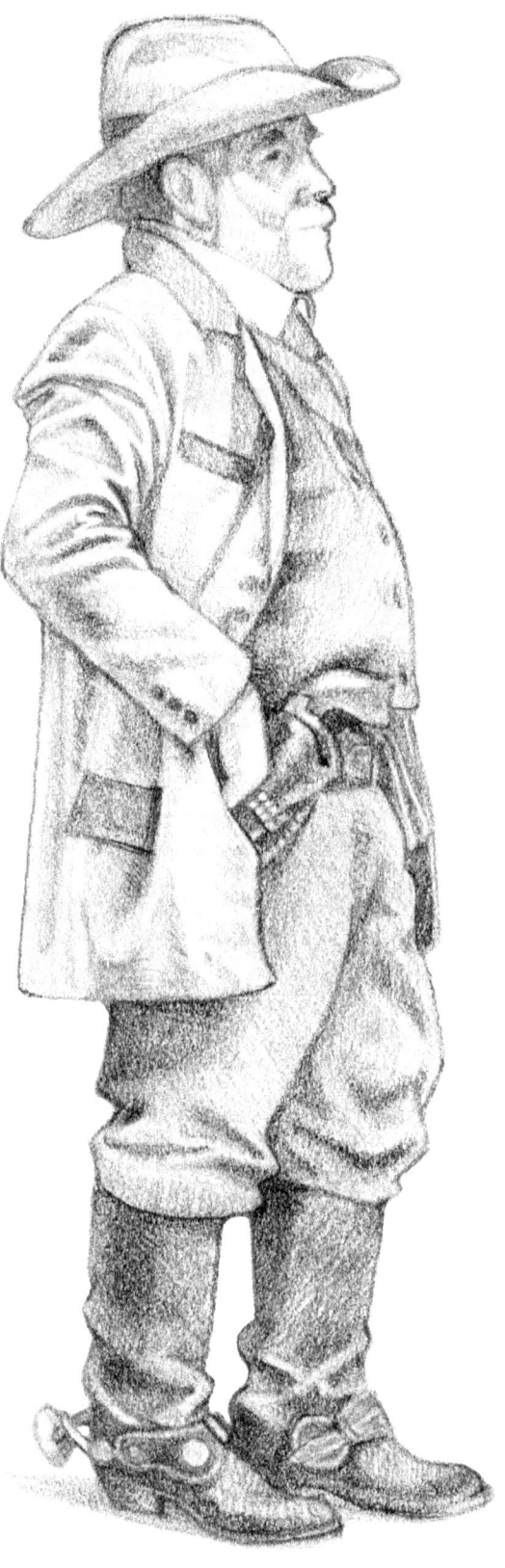

TYPES OF FOLDS

1. Pipe fold

This is the first type of basic fold. Almost every type of fold starts as a pipe fold in some way or another, even in its tiniest and most intricate form. The pipe fold we'll focus on specifically is the large pipe fold that is the result of fabric hanging from a point of gravity tension. As the fabric moves away from the point of tension above, it forms a tubular or pipe shape. When the pipe shape ends in midair, the results form the end of a cylindrical shape. Often, however, it'll hit a ground surface of some sort, onto which it will bunch upon itself in some way or another, redefining the final shape.

Pipe folds are generally cylindrical, and because of this, all of the rules about drawing and shading cylinders remain the same. You will have your core shadow on the rounded form of the cylinder. There may also be observable reflective light. You will also have a cast shadow of that cylindrical shape being cast back onto the fabric itself.

A basic example of pipe folds in action can be viewed in curtains. This is the easiest type of fold to observe and draw when you are beginning to practice folds.

Another place where pipe folds can be seen are in dresses. As the material falls away from the bunching that happens up around the waist, it'll fall to the ground in pipe folds. However, it often doesn't do this quite as nice and neatly as a simple curtain. You might observe that smaller pipe folds move away from where they are gathered and join together into larger pipe folds at a point that almost looks like a loop. This loop-like shape is a type of half-lock fold, which we will discuss later.

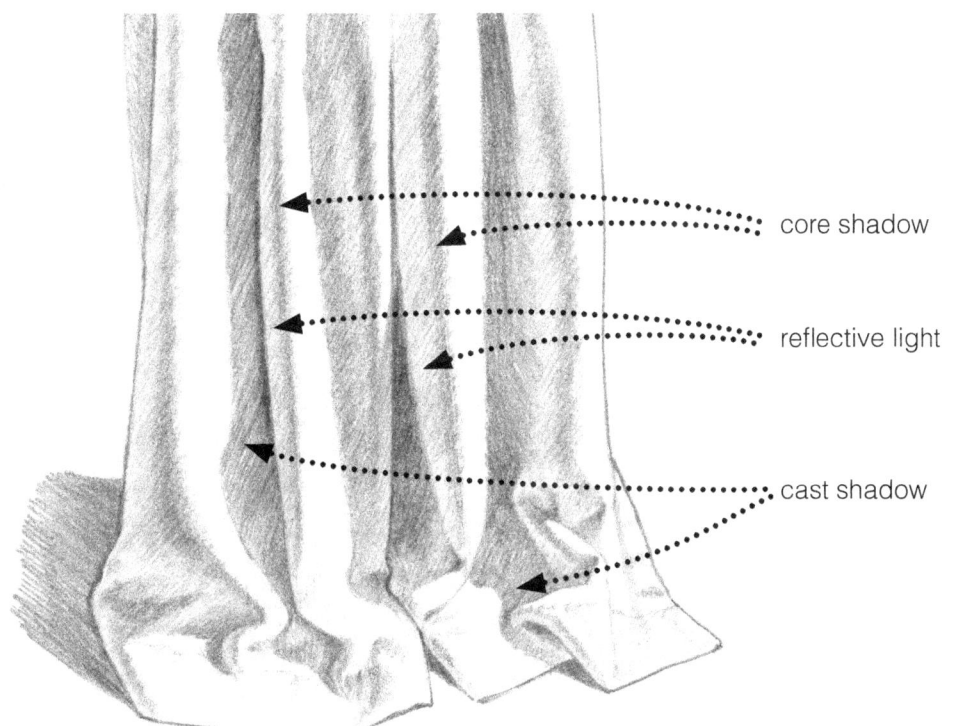

core shadow

reflective light

cast shadow

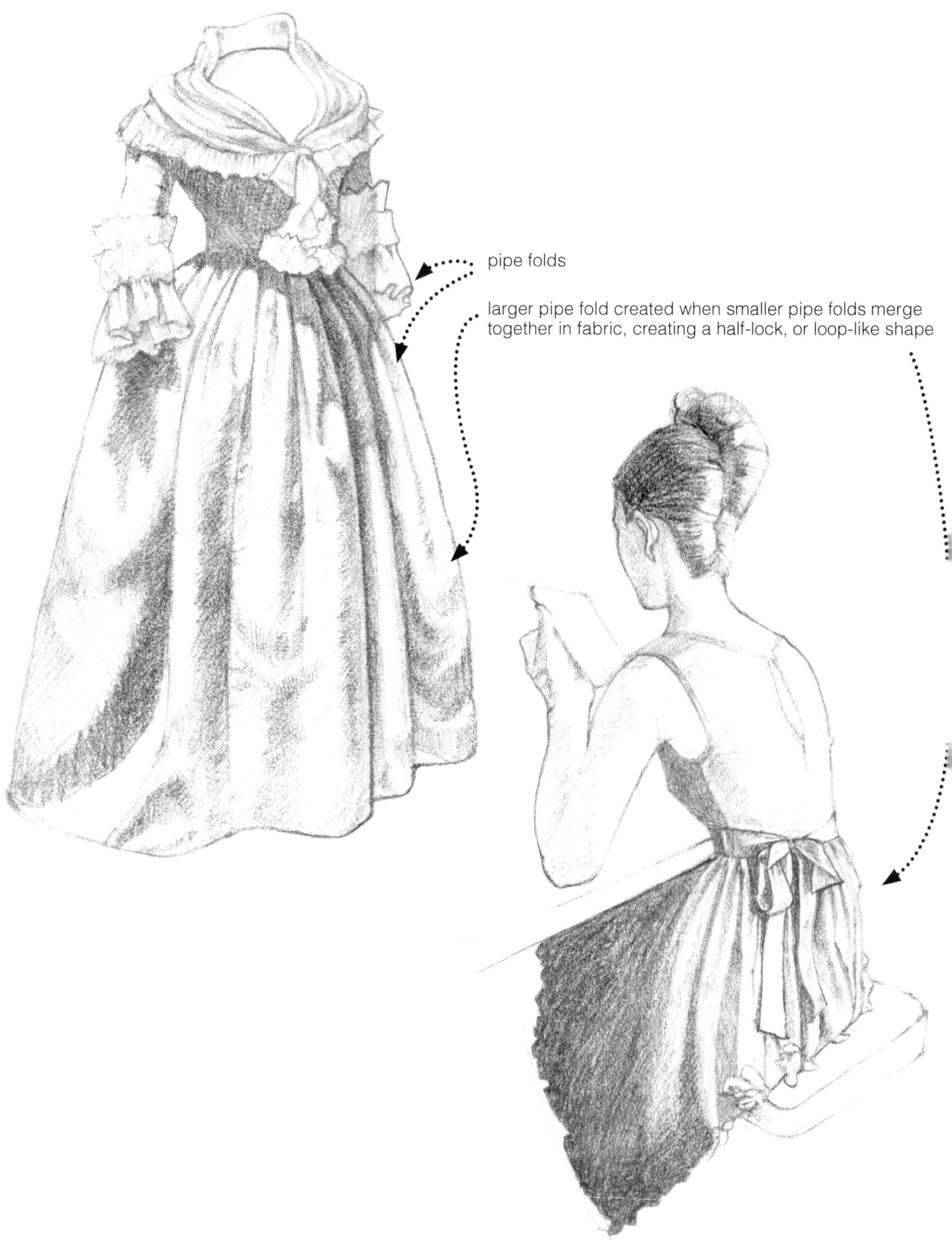

pipe folds

larger pipe fold created when smaller pipe folds merge together in fabric, creating a half-lock, or loop-like shape

2. Zigzag fold

This type of fold is the direct result of a bunch tension, and ties back into one of the earlier points I made about the interconnectivity of the fabric. It is because of this interconnectivity that we get the zigzag fold. As the fabric bunches together, the folds will appear to zigzag back and forth, forming these pockets of shadow between them. Sometimes a singular zigzag will appear, and sometimes there will be multiple zigzags as the fabric tries to find space as it's being compressed.

Here is what you need to remember about the zigzag fold.

First, it always follows the form. If the zigzagging occurs on an arm sleeve, remember the overall cylindrical shape of the arm. The folds will zigzag AROUND this shape, as you perceive it in perspective. This is very important. These are not arbitrary zigzags—they are very specific and they define the shape underneath.

Second, the folds of the zigzagging fabric need to connect. Now there may be some places of overlap where you cannot see where the connection occurs, that's fine. But where you can see the fabric and where it bunches up in a zigzagging pattern, look for where it connects as it moves back and forth.

Third, as the fabric connects back and forth with itself, the resulting inverted shapes are often tent-like or triangular shapes.

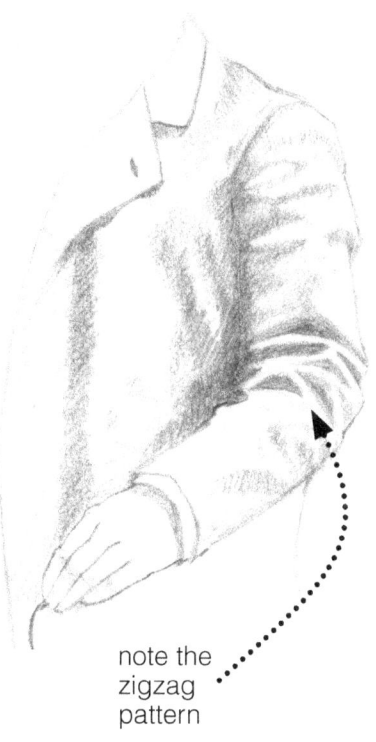

note the
zigzag
pattern

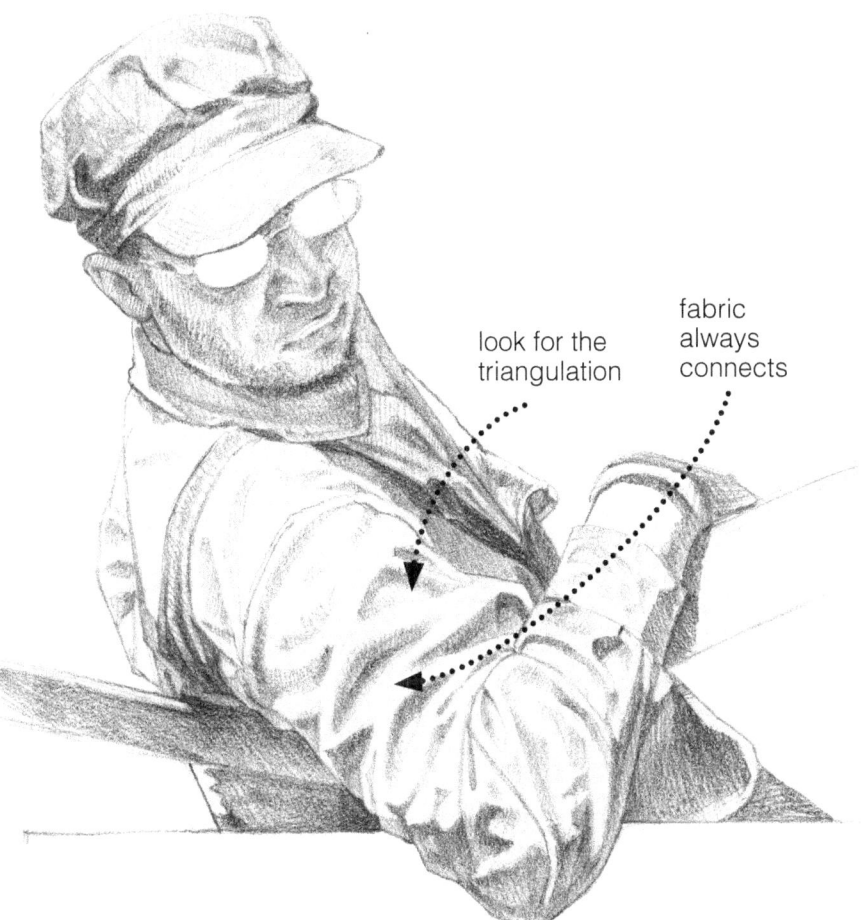

look for the
triangulation

fabric
always
connects

3. Spiral fold or radial fold

A spiral fold is usually caused by stress tension, but can be created by other forms of tension as well. You can see a spiral fold when fabric wraps around a tubular or cylindrical form, and there is enough tension to pull the fabric taut. The result is the appearance of a spiral or radiating effect of the fold lines as the folds ripple up and down the form.

This is especially observable if the cylindrical form is actually turned toward us, in perspective, such as an arm sleeve pointing in our direction. The more that cylindrical form is turned toward us, the more circular and rounded the folds become as they wrap around that shape. For example, artists often use a spiraling motion to enhance the action of sports figures, and frequently simplify the gestures of these folds with broad gestural radiating lines. When drawing these folds, start with circular lines that follow the form of the object underneath, and then find the folds on top.

Common places where one might see the spiral fold is rolled-up sleeves, too-tight tee-shirts, and oversized socks.

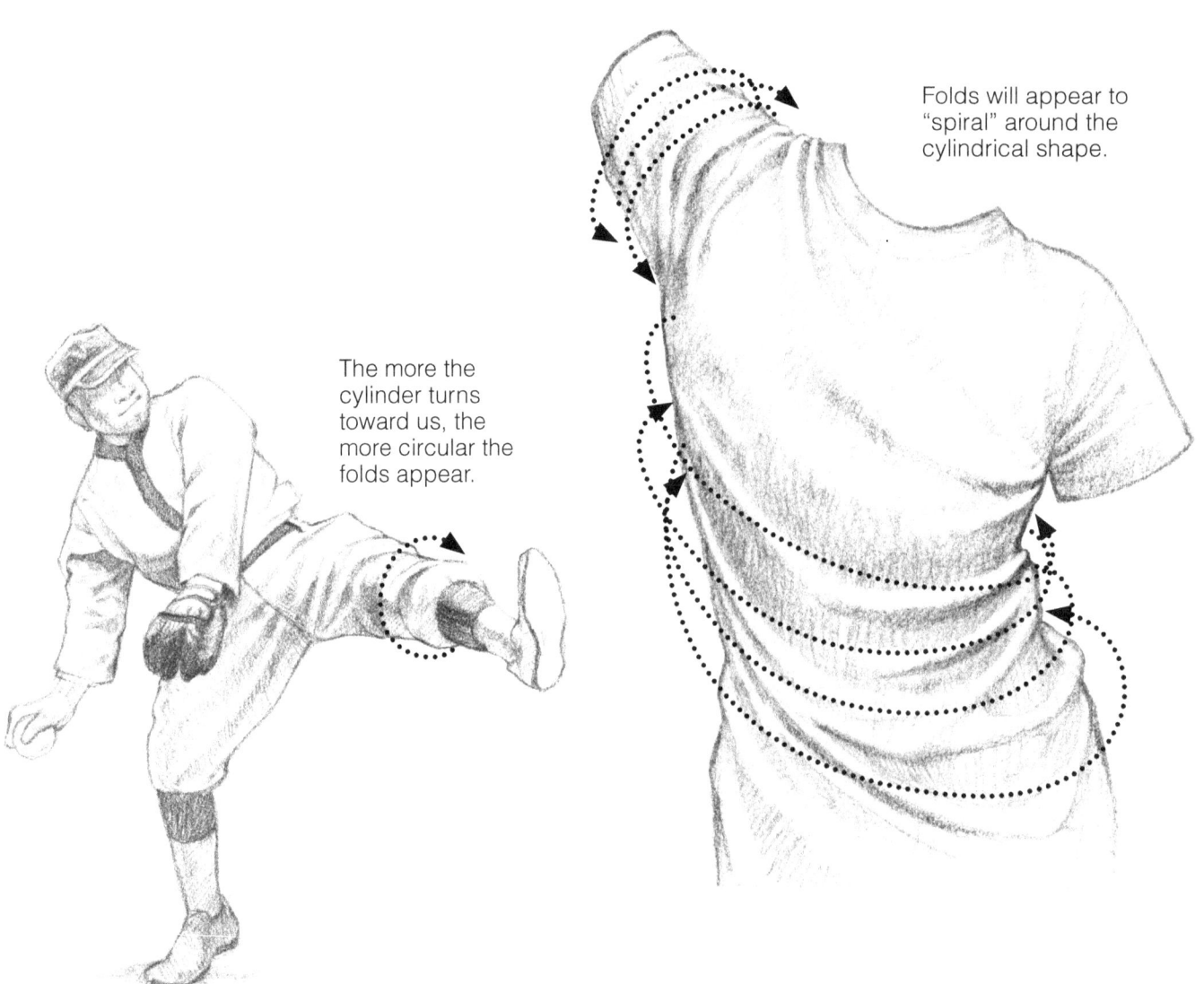

Folds will appear to "spiral" around the cylindrical shape.

The more the cylinder turns toward us, the more circular the folds appear.

4. Half-lock fold

In reality, we've already pretty much discussed the half-lock fold. It is nothing more than a singular zigzag fold or a pipe fold that changes directions. The fabric moves in one direction and then abruptly changes direction and moves in a different direction. Often you can see a pipe-like fold bending and becoming a cone shaped fold as it moves away from the bending point. The resulting shape in between is often triangulated.

Another type of half-lock fold is as we talked about with the pipe fold, where two smaller pipe folds join together into a larger pipe fold. Sometimes this joining together happens dramatically, and the triangulation that is the result is very observable. Other times, the coming together is softer, less dramatic, and the resulting shape appears as a loop.

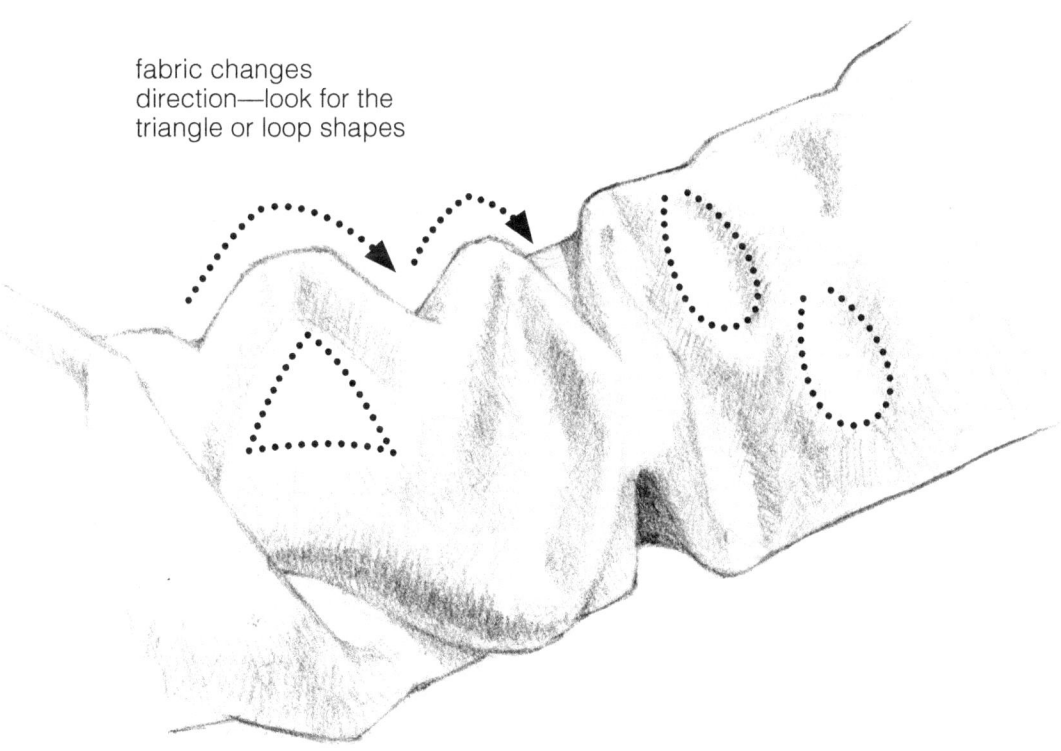

fabric changes direction—look for the triangle or loop shapes

5. Diaper fold

This is where you have two points of equal gravity tension. As a result, the folds swoop between these two points, forming bowl-like shapes. Remember to swoop your lines from one point of tension to the next, and look for those bowls. When it comes to shading, simply shade your bowl shapes like you would any basic bowl shape—the same rules of light and shadow apply. The rest of the fabric that falls away from the points of tension will do so as pipe folds.

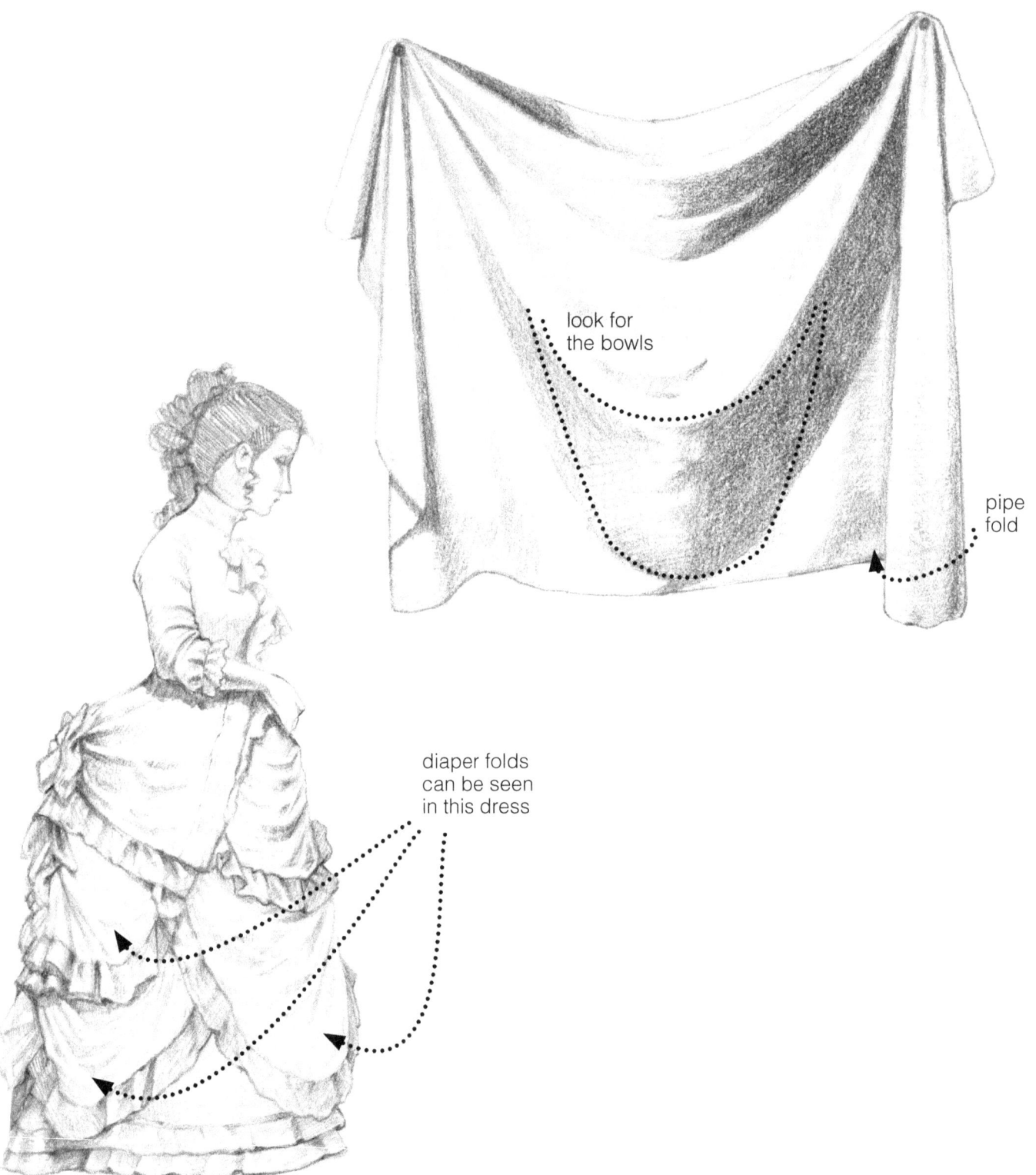

look for the bowls

pipe fold

diaper folds can be seen in this dress

6. Drop fold

Some instructional guides include a drop fold as a type of fold, describing it as fabric draped loosely over an object (remember the goose?). Everything that is the result of a drop fold is pretty much everything we have discussed so far in this teaching. When you throw a piece of fabric loosely over a form, you will have points of gravity tension, you will see pipe folds and half-lock folds, and the fabric will follow the form underneath. In essense, if you wanted to wrap up (*ahem*, pun partially intended) everything we've discussed in this book, there's probably no better way than to end with the so-called "drop fold." It is in essense the culmination of everything we've learned up to this point.

Now it's up to you to put it into practice. Go find yourself a ceramic goose, (or something similar), throw a pillow case on top and start drawing what you see.

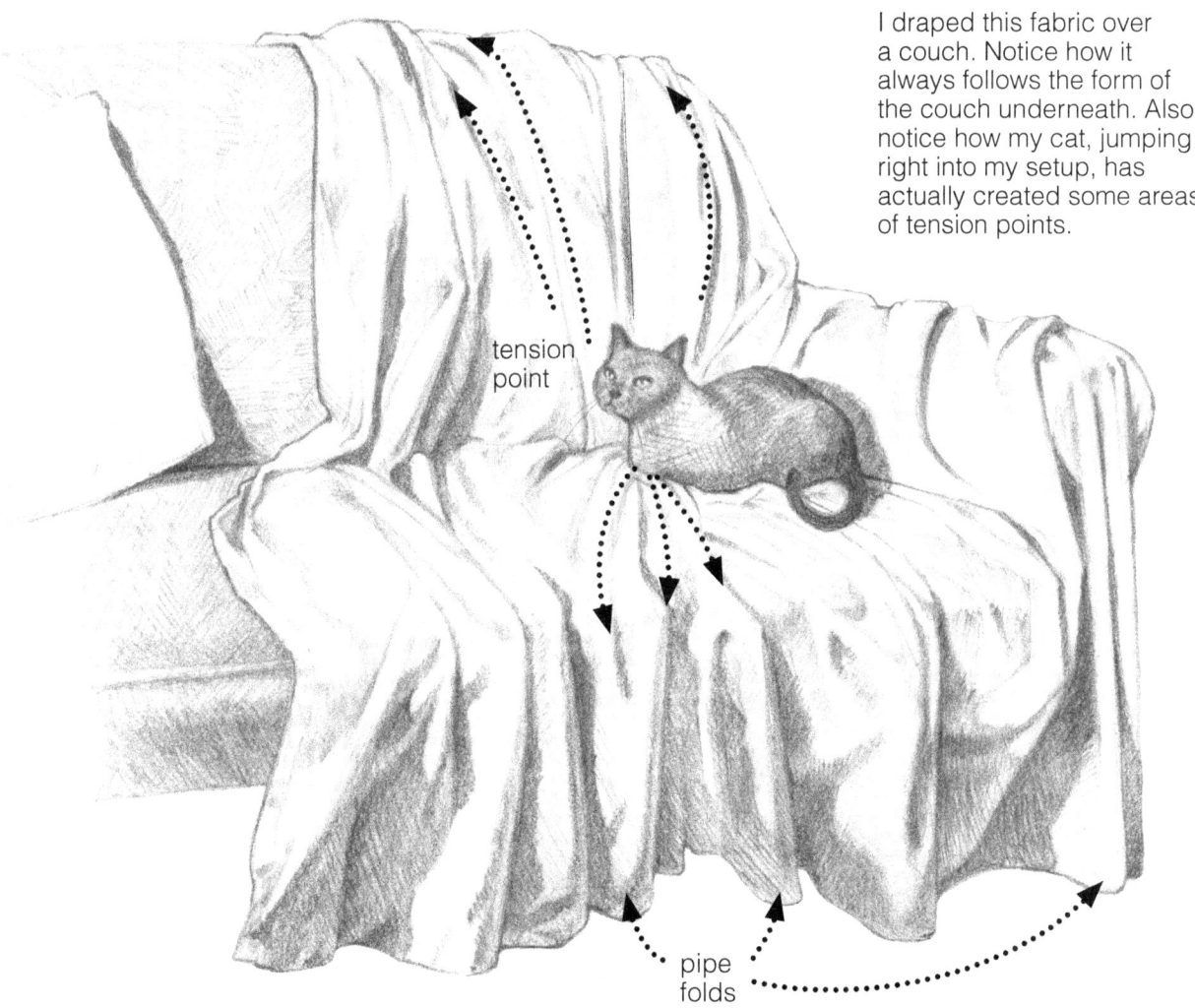

I draped this fabric over a couch. Notice how it always follows the form of the couch underneath. Also notice how my cat, jumping right into my setup, has actually created some areas of tension points.

tension point

pipe folds

IN CONCLUSION...

Hopefully this workbook has helped you understand how to see and draw folds a little more clearly. Once you comprehend the anatomy of folds and what to look for, they are no longer difficult and you can draw them realistically with ease.

Some photographs have been provided in the following pages for you to practice your folds. You may draw right in this workbook (unless you are borrowing this from a friend, in which case, ask first...), or feel free to practice in whatever sketchbook or paper surface you prefer.

We will start with the common drop fold. I've thrown a cloth over a small box to see what different kinds of folds appear. What we get is a unique abstract pattern of pipe folds and half-lock folds.

Key point to remember ... simplify. Look for the larger basic shapes first, observe how they connect to each other, and don't forget to pay attention to the form of the object that the fabric covers.

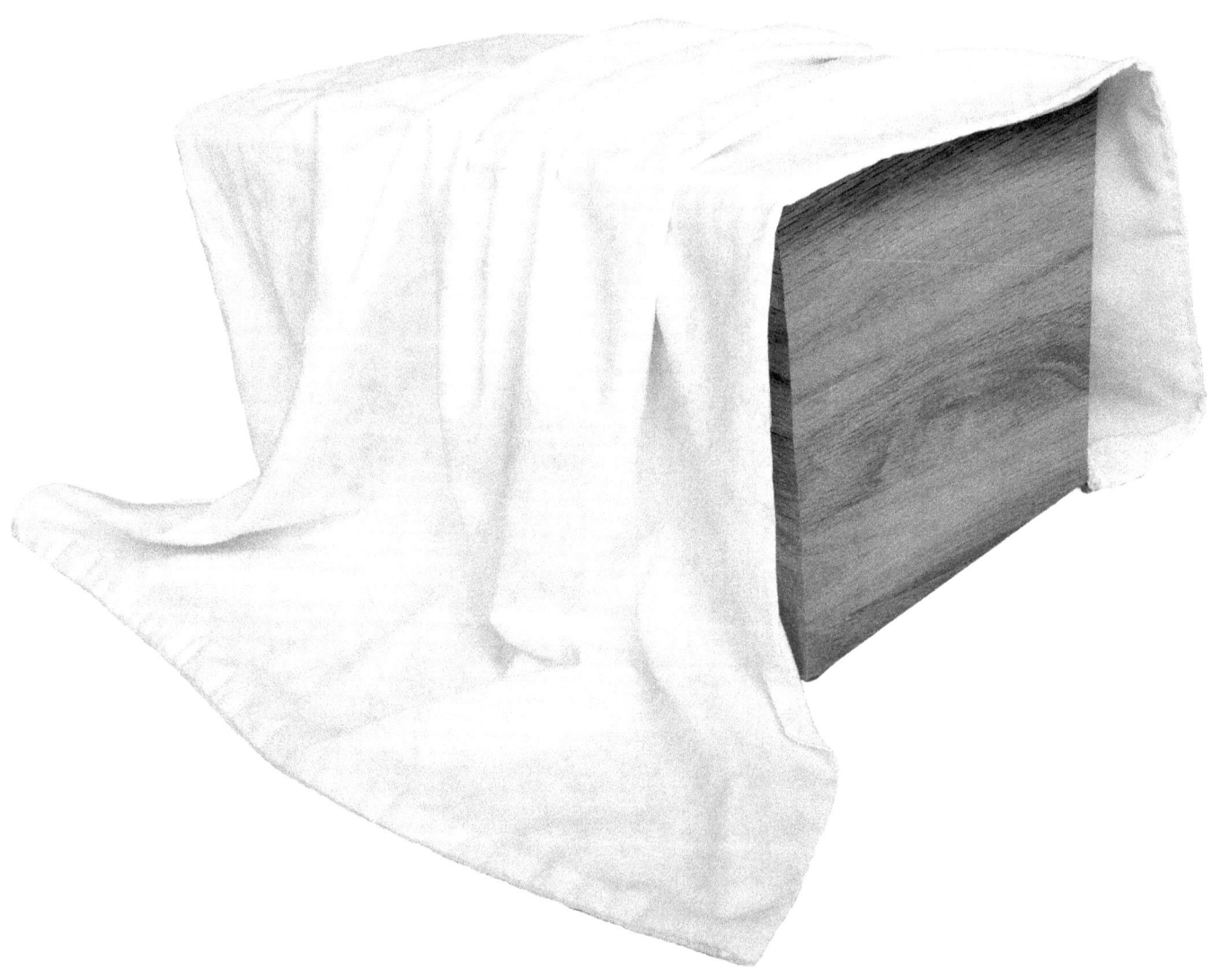

Show your work on social media!
See how others are drawing fabric, drapery and folds, and how they are using the instructions of this book to improve their work. Use the hashtag #HummelFoldsBook.

Can you draw the folds on a figure? This should be an easy one to get started with. A strong light source has been established. Remember to draw a definitive line around the shadow areas and don't forget to block them in boldly.

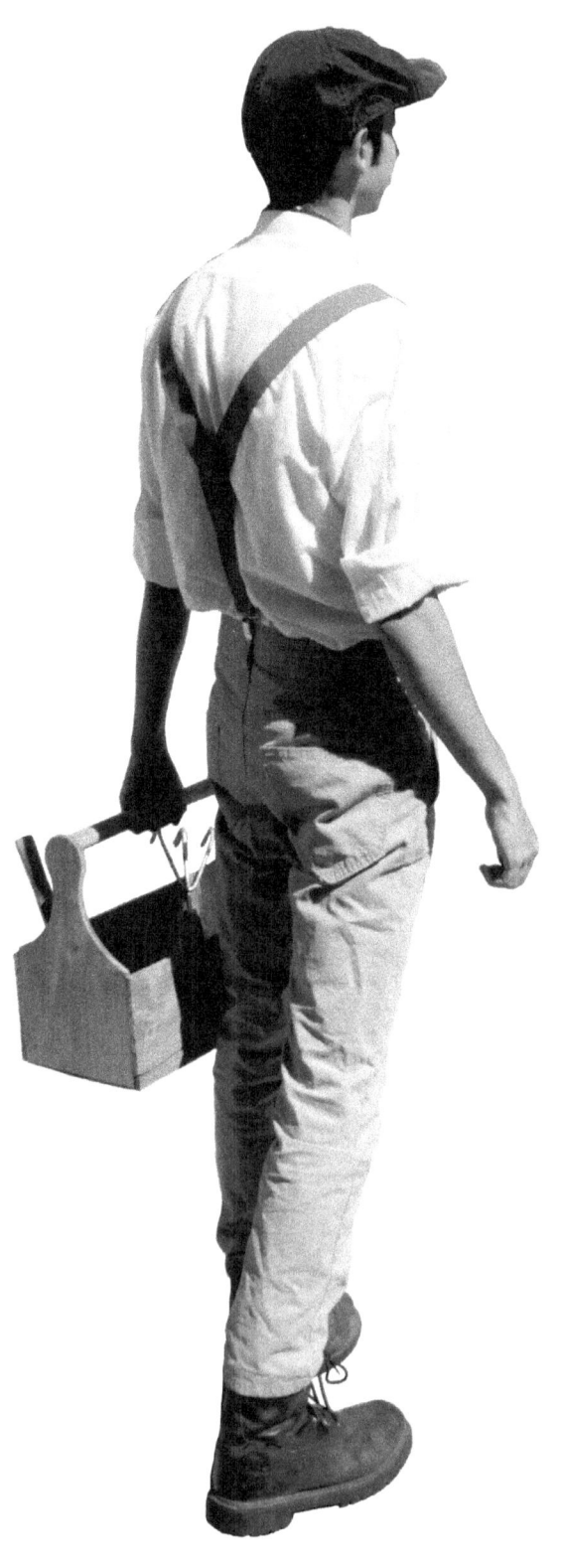

Show your work on social media!
See how others are drawing fabric, drapery and folds, and how they are using the instructions of this book to improve their work. Use the hashtag #HummelFoldsBook.

This photo is made up of mostly a series of pipe folds. Can you put them in correctly? Note their directional movement. Also, different types of fabric will behave slightly differently from each other.

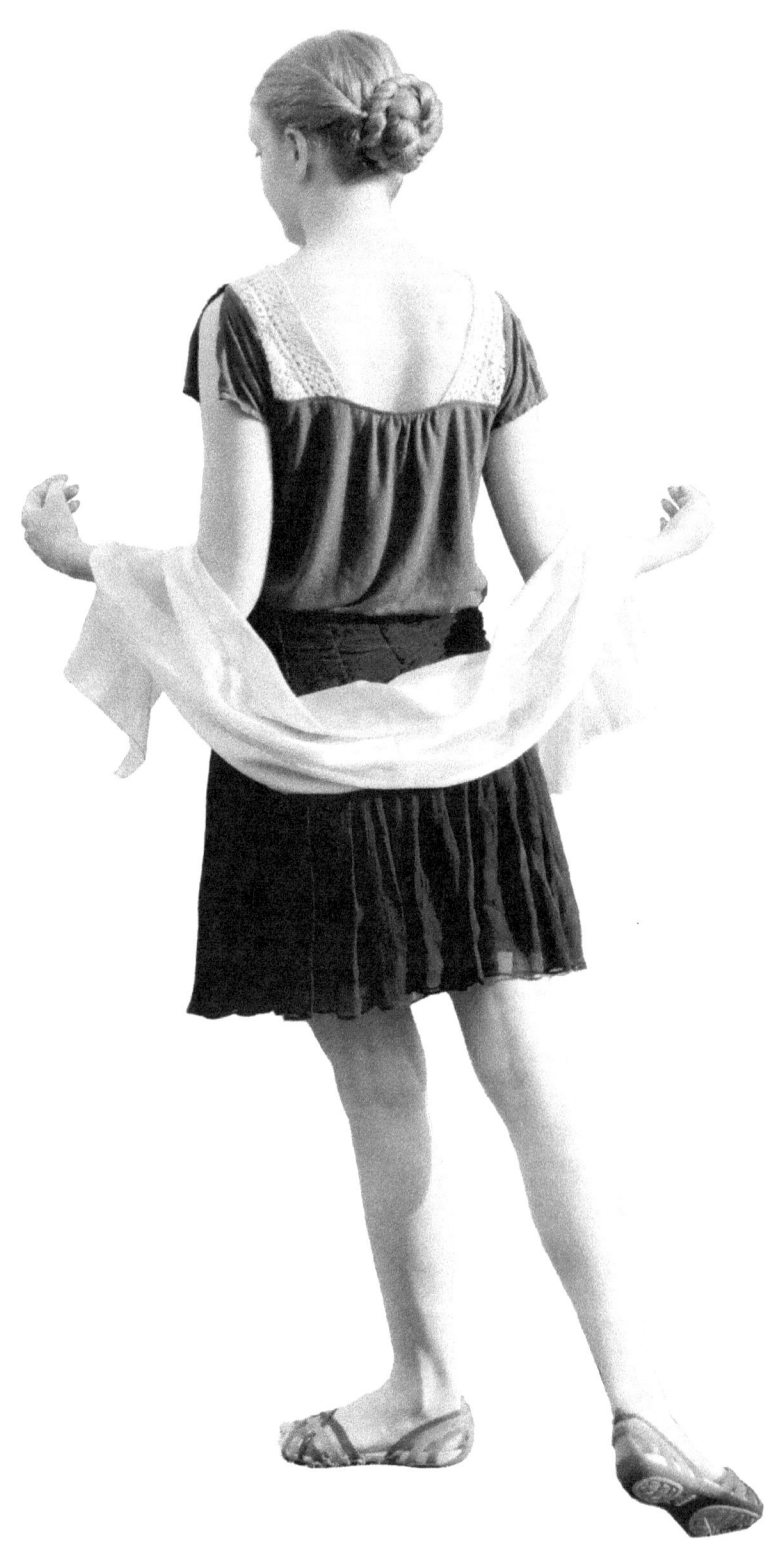

Show your work on social media!
See how others are drawing fabric, drapery and folds, and how they are using the instructions of this book to improve their work. Use the hashtag #HummelFoldsBook.

Your final challenge is this Greco-Roman sculpture, in which the folds have been artistically enhanced. Copying works by the great masters is a useful method to imporove your drawing skills.

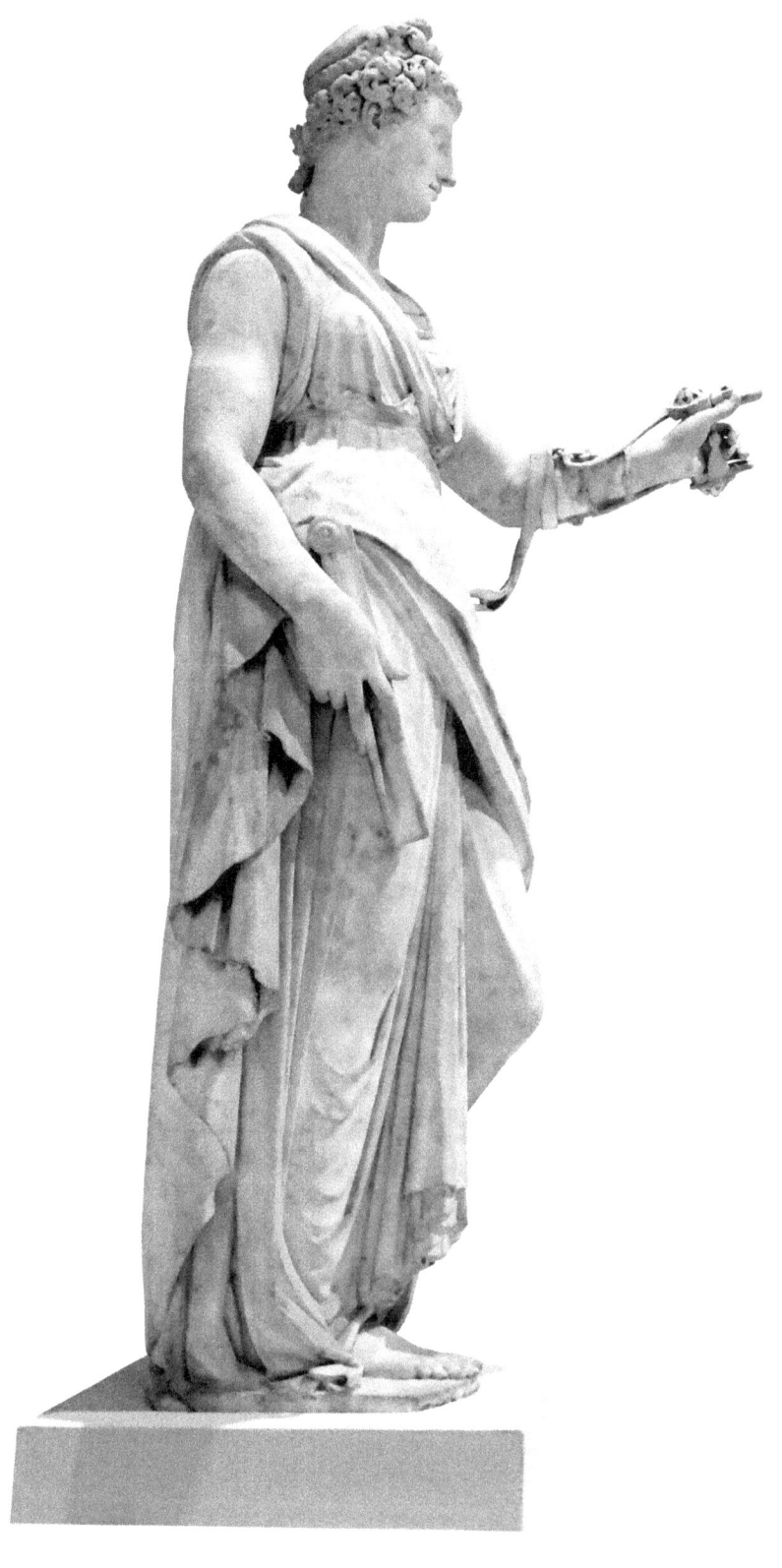

Show your work on social media!
See how others are drawing fabric, drapery and folds, and how they are using the instructions of this book to improve their work. Use the hash tag #HummelFoldsBook.

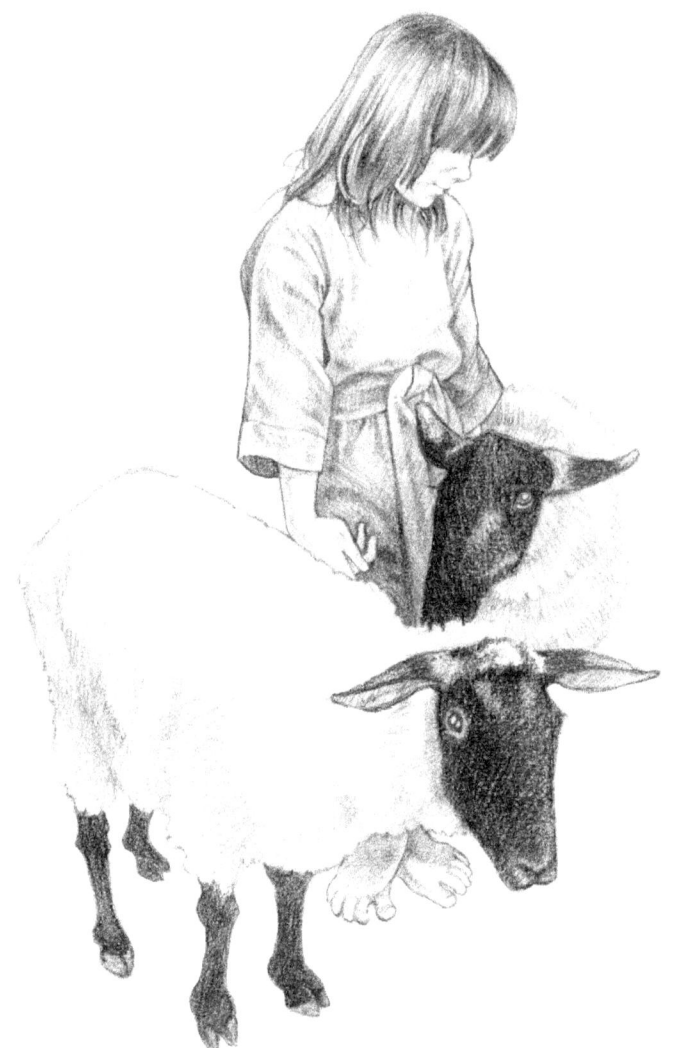

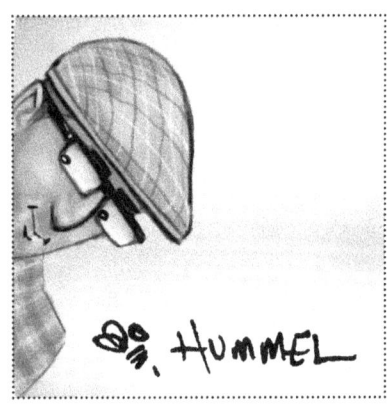

Benjamin Hummel's light-hearted illustrations have appeared in numerous children's books, textbooks, magazines, and greeting cards. However, his true passion is education. When he is not teaching at Rocky Mountain College of Art + Design, Benjamin writes books on drawing, illustration, and art. He is currently developing lessons on drawing hair and fur, drawing hands and feet, drawing children, and perspective drawing.

What makes Benjamin's story unique is the fact that he lives with a debilitating autoimmune disease which resulted in him receiving two liver transplants at the age of fifteen. As a result of his renewed lease on life, Benjamin dedicates his work to the joy of living. To overcome his daily physical challenges, he creates art that encourages others to live rich and full lives.

Benjamin documents his life, illustrations, process shots, and art tips on Instagram @hummelillustration.

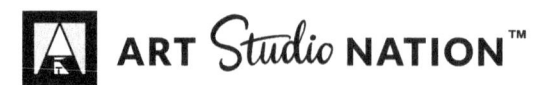

www.ingramcontent.com/pod-product-compliance
Lightning Source LLC
Chambersburg PA
CBHW081246180526
45171CB00005B/559